T0086051

CALL IT IN THE AIR

ALSO BY ED PAVLIĆ

Poetry

Let It Be Broke

Live at the Bitter End: A Trial by Opera

Let's Let That Are Not Yet: Inferno

Visiting Hours at the Color Line

But Here Are Small Clear Refractions

Winners Have Yet to Be Announced: A Song for Donny Hathaway

Labors Lost Left Unfinished.

Paraph of Bone & Other Kinds of Blue

Criticism

Outward: Adrienne Rich's Expanding Solitudes

'Who Can Afford to Improvise?': James Baldwin and Black Music, the Lyric and the Listeners

Crossroads Modernism: Descent and Emergence in African-American Literary Culture

Fiction

Another Kind of Madness

CALL IT IN THE AIR

poems

ED PAVLIĆ

MILKWEED EDITIONS

© 2022, Text by Ed Pavlić

All rights reserved. Except for brief quotations in critical articles or reviews, no part of this book may be reproduced in any manner without prior written permission from the publisher: Milkweed Editions, 1011 Washington Avenue South, Suite 300, Minneapolis, Minnesota 55415.
(800) 520-6455
milkweed.org

Published 2022 by Milkweed Editions
Printed in the United States
Cover design by Mary Austin Speaker
Cover photo/illustration by Kate Pavlich
Interior image of Mt. Shavano by David Herrera,
Creative Commons 2.0
Author photo by Sunčana Pavlić
22 23 24 25 26   5 4 3 2 1
First Edition

Library of Congress Cataloging-in-Publication Data

Names: Pavlic, Edward M. (Edward Michael), author.
Title: Call it in the air : poems / Ed Pavlić.
Description: First edition. | Minneapolis, Minnesota : Milkweed Editions, 2022. | Summary: "Somewhere between elegy and memoir, poetry and prose, Ed Pavlić's Call It in the Air follows the death of a sister into song"-- Provided by publisher.
Identifiers: LCCN 2021057231 (print) | LCCN 2021057232 (ebook) | ISBN 9781571315489 (paperback) | ISBN 9781571317674 (ebook)
Subjects: LCGFT: Poetry.
Classification: LCC PS3616.A9575 C35 2022 (print) | LCC PS3616. A9575 (ebook) | DDC 811/.6--dc23/eng/20220302
LC record available at https://lccn.loc.gov/2021057231
LC ebook record available at https://lccn.loc.gov/2021057232

Milkweed Editions is committed to ecological stewardship. We strive to align our book production practices with this principle, and to reduce the impact of our operations in the environment. We are a member of the Green Press Initiative, a nonprofit coalition of publishers, manufacturers, and authors working to protect the world's endangered forests and conserve natural resources. *Call It in the Air* was printed on acid-free 30% postconsumer-waste paper by Versa Press.

For Kate

. . .the desire to have a death of one's own is becoming more and more rare. In a short time it will be as rare as a life of one's own...

—RAINER MARIA RILKE,
The Notebooks of Malte Laurids Brigge

CALL IT IN THE AIR

Ca. 1972. The night's a blue spruce in my room   Dawn in my bed comes on green & silver in my mouth   You come in various ways You come in the middle of a dream to tell me about girls who eat their brothers   You tell me you have a friend no one knows about She's white as chalk   Veins slide across her bones like a tongue moves in moonlight   You tell me to picture it   Thin blue worms under my skin   She lives at the Ledge in the woods & helps women run away from the state prison

You say she chased you when you met & you jumped the stream
She broke her ankle & you heard it scrape on stone   She kept up
the chase   Her foot flopped like this   Your hand waves limp at
the wrist   The wet flap-flop end when you run thru puddles in
sock feet

You thru deep mud on the bank & her bone stuck in like a stake
The sole of her bare foot didn't look like hers   Turned over like a
black face turned clean-bone white & washed up chin-first out of
the mud

Denver I.C.U. Now. Here we sit. Surrounded by this

[   ]

Or are we invaded? A machine heaves your lungs open every
five or so seconds. Your new teeth in a jar, a tube cloth-taped to
your cheek. A metallic high tone it sounds like short bursts of air
going into an inner tube followed by the hiss of a punctured tire

It's like sitting next to a stranger in a movie while watching a kiss
in long silence both mouths open tongues a-swish in the dark.
After fifteen minutes I catch my breath waiting for yours. For the
machine. I try to tap my toe off beat & breathe on my own

Salida, CO. I sift your things. Maybe 2000 pieces of clothing from Good Will. I remember you called it "the free store." Almost doll-size, most of them on their improvised way back to being pieces of cloth. The rest you set on their quilted way back into use. Stained? Torn? Half-healed? This is a verb not a noun and it rhymes with if you search for moths and call it mothing: *cloth-ing*. They're all marked with some kind of paint or chalk, bits of other cloth sewn into them. A friend appears with a truck and we take a load of furniture back to the Good Will. A large woman with dirty blond hair informs us in preemptive tones: "We're not taking anything until next week." Tom is helping us. He knows this woman. He says, "Look, Linda, I don't know if you've heard, this is Kate's stuff; I don't know if you've heard that she died?"

"Kate? This is Kate's stuff? Overdose, right?"

Tom and Linda look at me with cut eyes. He says, "This is her brother." No visible sign from me. I have the syringe from under the driver's seat of your jeep in my bag. Later I'll put it back under the seat. Then Mom and I cleaned out your jeep. And now the syringe is gone as if it wasn't ever there.

Ca. 1972. A summer night feels like it feels when I wake to the golden ends of your hair along the slope of my spine. A summer night feels like it buried my breath hot into the cool pillow. Your breath on the back of my arm. A summer night feels like it feels to the first hands in the room on my walking stick's worth of a nude undercovers body. You sing There's no time to hold a spark. You say Hurry up dreary deary you have to learn where to touch yourself before you blink & disappear in the dark   .

Denver I.C.U. There are ten rhythms on the screen over your shoulder. I see graphs. I know the area under the slope of the line is the good news. I know there's a button to invert the program. I have one on my stereo. Basslines. I see points that jog in sync with different metabolic functions. One's blood-in, one's blood-out.

There's a pie chart for what percentage of air the machine's putting into you at each heave. A fantastic apparatus. I hold on to cold chrome & let the room twirl around the rhythm of the only lie left in your bottomless bag of tricks: breath.

I go behind the desk to make a phone call and find a big screen with readouts from the patients on the floor. Names written on scraps of cloth tape: Abrams, Gentry, Mendez. . . Pavlich, Xiao. . . I go to the thumbnail for Pavlich: dots dance, lines bump & start, there's the pie chart for oxygen into that thing they're calling your breath. I've seen the arrow buttons to the side of the pie. One points up, one down. It's work. This is someone's job. This is someone's sister. This is someone's life. And someone's death.

I blur my eyes like you taught me to do: "Try to focus on something inside your eyeball. . ." The names go away & I think, one of these cipher-sets is my big sister? One of them is someone's brother. Does Mendez have a brother? Maybe. You taught me, Kate, inside-out, what a big sister means. The rest is apparatus. I've no sound in my body for the arm of a brother. My brothers all came later. From elsewhere.

The nurse turns to me and her mouth moves. She chews her tongue and I read her lips. She tells me that the machines breathe for my sister. I told her that is a lie. My lips don't move. It's not her fault.

And I wonder if there's a person alive who knows how to expect & remember the warmth of Xiao's weight, her calf curled around his leg? Or hers. Spoons in a drawer. The taste of pollen caught in her eyelash. The owner of a sable shadow falls off the sheer slope of her face and moves across a sky of bent wooden slats in an uneven floor. Her hands are the color of the sound of a broom, sunlight swept up in an empty room.

Ca. 1972. You'd come back & I'd cry   Your eyes look like two Zippos held open above me   You say your eyes are the frayed ends of empty sleeves   You muffle me   You say death & the flame-eyes change color   You say death is a thing that happens every time your sweat touches someone you don't know who you're supposed to know   You'd lie down on top of every inch of me & tell me there's nothing I can do   You say people change every time they leave a room

Ca. 1972. The ceiling gathers up into heavy points of steel on the ends of pins & you say don't bother asking mom about your chalk-colored friend   Cause mom wouldn't help her & so she hates mom   The day you double-rode me out there & we hiked   It wasn't a hike   She wanted to see me   You say   She watched thru the trees as we hiked up the trail to The Ledge

She cleans her teeth with sticks & chews the gum   She lives out there all night in the dark   She scrubs her bare arms with dry pine cones   She smells like this   Your knees pin my arms   A tuft of hair brushes the tip of my nose   A hush   When she moves she sounds like wind and broken sticks   She wipes herself with the ash of burnt oak leaves & she smells just like this   hush   this here

Denver I.C.U. When I come back in the room there is a dry, red streak from the corner of your eye. Here we sit while a machine jerks open your lungs. I know your breath. The nurse says the machine helps you breathe. I smile and shake my head. I mean it. My head doesn't move. It's not her fault. Mom told me about when you were four and you sat across from her and told her you knew how to start crying. You laughed & I know you looked straight into her eyes & I know she doesn't know how you looked at her. I know that sweat, that fear. I've seen you when you're purely you— Mom tells me you sat there and stopped laughing and then tears came. Then you stopped smiling & made your face the face that starts to cry.

And I knew because I'd seen you empty your face of everything you didn't want me to see. I'd seen it love. I'd seen it pleasure. I'd seen it terror. Pure. I'd seen you smelt the elements. I'd heard you scream and scratch and bite, pure. I knew you had a friend that watched me whenever I was alone, I knew she'd trap me in the woods and she'd sing that song and eat me for dinner.

I'm your little brother. That means your hands are inside me. I look up & see my tiny big sister who taught herself how to cry. In this I.C.U. room you look like a baby bird that fell from its nest. Your hand opens & I take a—whatever they call it—breath of whatever they call this:

[   ]

I say squeeze my hand and you do it once. You opened your eyes
to see if I know anything about this. You surfaced back into your
eyes once. Held my hand once. Do I know about this? Up to a
point, Kate. Ok? Up to a point.

The light brown in your eyes has gone speckled green. The whites
just gone into lakes of red & everything in your eyes is straight
ahead. The periphery's gone. The intern's comatose. It's not his
fault. The nurse murmurs about platelets as the blood wells up. I
sit with a tissue, dizzy-ready.

I know they're not tears, Kate. At the same time, these aren't your eyes. The nurse holds your lids open and I see eyes someone put there. You did that. You've given away your breath to people who move their lips without talking. Your eyes are acts of pure will. Surrounded in this room, they're *only* human. A razor-straight road thru the Rockies. They stare out like a jet leaves an only-human scar in the sky.

I hate to fly because I hate and fear the only-human. The straight. The cruel efficiency. But once we're in the air...

An innate talent for terrified fearlessness. Yours. Eyes full of blood stare at me. Yours. Stare thru me. There are people here whose job is to be *only* human. Never to be looked at, they speak without speaking.

There's still your involuntary warmth, Kate. Your hand in mine got here by avoiding pain at all cost. But there's only one way to avoid the warmth.

In an angry letter to a friend on May 27, 1927, Hart Crane: "My 'alert blindness' was a stupid ambiguity to use in any definition– but it seems to me you go in for just about as much 'blind alertness' with some of your expectations."

Here's a red tear from your eye.

Self-taught means you either taught yourself or you just always knew how to start, Kate. & I know, by death, it means you never let anyone offer you the first tip about how to stop.

Near Buena Vista, CO. It was the last time I came to see you before this time. I didn't know then. Now, I can see the deal you two had made. You and Tim. I waited for you at the airport for 6 hours. You said it took most of the day before, by luck, you were both awake at the same time. After that, you say, "We left right away."

We stopped in Manitou Springs for lunch. Chips, salsa, and margaritas. Tim couldn't walk straight. His hands shook and you both agreed on the lie of Parkinson's. At home, he paddled around with a cane you'd made him, on a stool you'd rigged with wheels. You lived together within arm's reach of the tree line, halfway up Mt. Yale from Buena Vista.

I sat on his pine deck at somewhere around ten thousand feet
with a huge white lip between me and a deep blue wave coming
over the ridge a few thousand feet further up. Late April sun
hotter than July on my face, January air plunges down over
a million tons of snow & ice. The cloudless sky's an invisible
frenzy. The sun and the wind blow under loose denim & play
on my body like a match on gas spilled across a frozen lake. I
brought asthma, cigarettes I'm afraid to smoke and *The Literary
Correspondence of Hart Crane and Yvor Winters*. I'd borrowed the
book from Jordan. I figure Crane's the sun & the wind, both. And
Winters is the lip of ice.

The first night. I go to bed when you two are about to wake up. You scream that you don't care, about something, the first something, second and something else and tires peel in the gravel. I look out and the stars aren't in the sky. They're bolts of light stuck straight into the ground. Tim raves about you and about knives and I remember the collector's edition blades he has framed on the walls of this house.

I've read that Beretta is the longest-lived industrial firm on Earth. Under my bed there's a left-over piece of iron railing. I'm worried about my wind at this altitude and my grip when my hands sweat. I worry about leaping from the roof & impaling myself on stakes of starlight.

I glance around the corner and there Tim sits, shrieking about his knife, rowing himself in a circle on his stool with an empty bottle of Black Label in his lap.

So, there it is: I see the deal you two made: death by your own hands. And I'm no longer worried about the bolts of star-chrome in the road.

The next day you cook Tim lunch. He's watching *Fight Club*. He's on about you: "I love your sister, but she's so fucking weird; I love your sister, but she's so fucking weird." My teeth on edge I tune him out until I hear "bitch" and then I'm packing all your shit into the jeep and we're gone by five. I've got three days left here. I figure two days cleaning your place. *Christ*, Kate. On the third, you say you want to climb with me up to the Angel.

I say that's not your life in his house and it's not your death there either. I say that's *his* death up there if he wants. You nod at the ground. Smoke curling around your ears. I say there's nothing up there. You nod and say you never wanted to paint him. As a distraction you used his socks to paint his porch, deck, kitchen, stairs. Never him not even a stroke in a sketch. You say you know I'm right because you can only see him with your eyes open.

& I say the state of your apartment in town confesses your insides. You turn to me & nod. I could but I don't and I still don't know. That body and that off-limits intensity you live inside. That blurry wheeling—common enough—pulsed by a—strange and truly rare—skill with otherworldly clarity.

I hadn't then. I have now. In your diary of two written pages and endless sketches of faces, shapes and faces pouring out of other faces and into shapes that are also faces: Friday May 7, 2004, you write:

"I've been up for 36 ½ hours---not by choice (also havn't been home in this last day. I was up visiting Tim, at Game Trail, no sleepy no sleepy-------I wish Tim would just ask me to marry him! I could love him with (at least I believe no nasty shit happening!"

Salida, CO. In your apartment in town, I fold & fold & hang
clothes & uncover paintings & burritos & pyramid-shaped empty
bottles of Pátron & an ad hoc anthology of vibrators. "Just throw
any of those you find over there," you say, "no, give me that purple
crook-fingered one." You put the purple one in your back pocket.
I've folded clothes and cleared a path to the bathroom. There's
an antique chair with the caning ripped out of the seat over the
toilet and a TV of vast, obscene scale against the wall. The TV is
almost the room.

I take a seat & you come in: "Look, I don't care what he said
about me," waving a bent purple vibrator at me, "But, if he's going
to call my brother names, I'm not talking to him. That's it." I
hadn't heard the names. After you're dead I asked around, Kate. I
couldn't resist. No one saw you two together after I left.

Denver I.C.U. The nurse called it a grave condition. A doctor told me that you were a young woman with a dead liver. No one needed to tell me why you weren't on the transplant list. No one knows. It's not their fault.

Everyone waited for me to ask. Everyone needs to tell me why you're not on the transplant list. They don't know why they're right about that. I know they're right about that but they don't know that *that's* why. It's their job to tell me they do. It's in their stance. They're ready for me to object. To argue, to resist. To object: I know that accent is on the first syllable. The nurses and doctors don't know that. It's not their fault. I won't argue, demand reasons. I've long known there are no reasons. It doesn't matter. Their job isn't to know why. I won't *óbject* you Kate. Their job isn't to know why, it's to tell me why. It's a grave situation. In grave situations, I learn, it's important to listen & listen & not to let the things said get in the way of what I hear.

Your life was a distilled assault on the foundations beneath any reason for anything. During those years when you were blind, after three weeks in your new trailer with Deke, you returned from the crawl space to announce: "There's half a car under our house, but I can't feel enough of it to know what kind it is."

Salida, CO. When you're dead, I go to "the Vic." I see Deke. He says, "Sorry for your loss." He means it and I appreciate that. I ask him, "how long were you two married, five years? He says, "twelve," and takes his beer back to the pool table. I could have known that. I didn't. I do. I sit and stare at your only publicly exhibited piece of art. A ventriloquist's puppet of the owner of the bar, Peter. He sits at the end of the rail. His twin hangs by strings in his trophy chest at the back. The Victoria Tavern & Hotel, 143 F Street, Salida, Colorado.

The Angel of Mt. Shavano,
May, Chaffee County, Colorado

In Beckett's "Rough for Theater II," three men. One poised for a fatal leap from the window. The other two, one suspects, a little less than really there, enter up stage and take seats in school desks behind the first. They're to account for the man's past as he leans out the window, his future prospects if any. The two are there to add up and subtract a life. One accountant carries a folio. In the folio, a number of file folders each with a category of information about the man's life. The two have come to review the file. Misspelled.

Denver I.C.U. The nurses here are well-behaved and better trained than that. One wears a cross and holds my hand a second too long in hers. The angle in her brow just one notch too many to the puppy-dog side of things to do what she's trained to do for me. But that's *me*. Far as that goes she seems perfect for *you*. There's useful care in her trained touch. How different from mine: untrained, blind with love and dizzy-sick with everything. I sit still while eleven bodies of mine fall all over the countless mysteries of who you are determined to be. There's the soup-skinned, the tangle-toothed, ivory-threaded, hand-blown glass-ribbed, the spent .38 slug-brained and the box-in-one squad trying to guard them. Then the real me, with no mouth who watches the whole thing, as if from above. You trust him?

The doctors seem well-read. Two of them are precisely articulate.
The intern's comatose. It's not his fault. In a few minutes,
we're going to leave you here in the I.C.U. dock and meet in a
windowless conference room to talk about how long you're going
to live, misspelled. I know my job is to destroy false foundations
such as the tense of the previous sentence. I'm here to guard
your death. They're going to ask me if I want a cup of coffee.
Before they lead us off to discuss the lines on the screen, the
renal specialists arrive. Out on his feet, the intern nods into a
stainless, wheeled table and a stack of metal pans on the floor
dance in a bright flame of silence. Seems the kidney numbers
have improved. The young professional in lab whites, patting his
superior and himself on the back with the same hand, says "seems
we've reversed" the. . . some Latinate phrase that means damage
to otherwise healthy kidneys that accompanies liver failure.
They call the condition "end stage" liver disease. Two days ago,
everyone thought the twin liver / kidney failure, coupled with
the pneumonia, would kill you in spite of the corna-technia that
surrounds us. The specialists jot a few figures in their pocket
notebooks and swish off on their thin-soled leather loafers.

[   ]

43

The older specialist speaks with a German accent. His English comes from his mouth with something just less than a glance of ironic precision. He discusses my sister's round-robin of terminal conditions while I wonder what disaster accounts for the complex of shadows that scurry beneath his tongue. Specialist the Younger, a New Englander, speaks English like an unfortunate inheritance, like the language is a trust fund forced upon him by cruel and boring fate. His forehead sun-browned behind thin golden hair.

I think "young professional." I think, he's a golfer. I tell them I appreciate their work for my sister and I do. We talk without talking. Work. I think you'd have liked to talk with the older doctor alone. Maybe dash a study or two, thumb in pastels, if he was buying at the bar, or charcoal if he was passing thru. I want to tell the Younger that my sister couldn't have done half a decent job wiping her ass in the time it'd have taken her to notice him, size him up, and forget she'd noticed him.

I felt like saying, "ten minutes of my sister's waking life would have burned you down to a handful of cinders." I didn't, of course, say: "One of her five-year-old dreams would swallow you whole and spit out the seeds." Not exactly the time for it. But, the real reason for my appreciative silence was that I knew it was impossible to speak for you, Kate. Chances are, in half a study-sketch, you'd have revealed the hidden lives led by these two and reversed my impressions. Or not. I kept my blind mouth shut.

44

The news: the kidneys aren't going to kill you, Kate. The liver's
dead in the water and there's no living long without it. It's not
his fault. The intern snaps awake, closes his eyes and confides:
"she's not a candidate for transplant." So we thank one hand for
washing the other and walk off to talk about whether we should
help you die now or set you up to go through it all and bleed-
out again somewhere soon and die all over again on your own.
The specialists are game for the challenge. I keep sensing I'm
surrounded.

[   ]

Salida, CO. The roof of your jeep must be up on the mountainside near the tree line in Tim's garage. We're not going back for it. The night before we go to the Angel, we drive up to Leadville and back looking for orange and blue thread you need for something you have to do immediately. A custom-made margarita in a stainless coffee mug in your hand: "I told him it needed more Grand Marnier." I drove. Somewhere along the way, heat blasting past us & out the open jeep, the mountain sky turned to black steel & swung open its empty mouth. The line of your face pushed against the tongue of the night. The air tastes blue & plays our heads like cold flame. The dark line of your face pushes into bright black steel. A shut-eyed face hidden by a night wing. A serrated song with a split tongue of onyx feathers.

In your eyes, I could see the terror of the night, pure as a sable coat filled with smoke. I think to myself as I look at you: she's not going home from here. This is home for her. This wide-open jeep flung however into a steel-black sky. I think, I wouldn't last five minutes in her skin. Without moving, you lean into it. Closer. You say there's a tunnel with no walls, faces appear like fireworks, one streams from another. You say just above our heads, you see a face that calls us from where the first person joins the last. You say the sky's a black, bottomless pond and we're stones and our home's in that depthless depth, these lives are puny circles, ripples on the face of the pond. You say you met a man named Dan with exactly *that* face under a crushed felt hat at a bar in Cripple Creek one night four years ago. You tell me you sketched a quick study of his face and asked his number. You say it started with area code 303 and so you figured what's the point? You never saw him again.

Going through your stuff I found:

"Untitled," Kate Pavlich, Undated

There's art each day. I used to believe that images worked like damp sponges, drew from experience & gave it a texture. On May 27, 1927, Hart Crane wrote an angry letter to a close friend. Crane burnt the letters his friend wrote back. Crane wrote: "You think that experience is some commodity that can be sought. One can respond only to certain circumstances, just what the barriers are, and where the boundaries cross can never be completely known."

& so I wonder openly what *experience* has to do with daily life? & is art a mobile barrier or a crossed boundary? Or both?

Upstate NY. These days I cut my hands open at home on purpose. I don't know why I do it. On the back of my *asdf* hand, seven cuts in the skin like notches on a pistol handle trace the bone that leads to my index finger. I need help and there's no help. I need grief and can't touch the skin of the word. I need work and there's no damned work to do. You're dead and the sky's empty on my open face. I feel compelled to respond to things beyond the boundary and I've been invaded by hands I can't touch. I need my sister breathing on this planet. I have a job and I do it. I need my sister's breath in this sky. My job: come up with a way to rescue the day from oblivion. Surprising results. Through an unlikely series of accidents, I lean over and touch my son's face. Every day I invent my work from scratch & every time I notice a few things aren't where I left them the day before.

I do this in upstate NY. And the results orbit me, maybe, as I exist in a crowded, everyday space of unimaginable isolation.

I cry because family means in everything we do. I cry because families have almost nothing to do with us. When I imagine my father talking to me & he becomes someone he's not, I cry. He won't talk. I'll invent him & fail. I've just done it. & failed. The facts of life. He's spent his life working instead of talking. At least to me. &, likely, I'm wrong. I cry when I realize I don't wish for conversations with him. The fact that he was away my whole life, the horror of never missing him. Of never knowing what to miss or if I should. His horror of not being missed. Silent. And I have two kids. Where are they? (Which means where, which means what, and who—am I?) Then I glance down at my hands; there he is. I've got *his* hands. He sent the money home every week, spent before it had a stamp. He's seen this in my eyes. When he's here, he's here. When he's not here. He's not here. I cry when I think it's fine like it is. It isn't. The facts of life. It's "brick," no matter how many there are, the word is singular. I know that and I have no memory of learning that.

My father can tell you, within a few thousand, how many brick it takes to build a man. But, he can't relay the location of this man.

Show me the line between work and life? The barrier between pain that builds and pain that tears away. Veins of pain in the brick. Invisible lines of human presence in the air. There are no final reasons on a screen that prevents our fall, into the endlessly anonymous patterns that spell our names. My sister's testimony—who could tolerate it?

The endless faces that appeared before my sister's eyes. There are thunder heads that weigh more than a battleship.

Light is a murderous lie about the bottomless weight of the dark. Pearly-wet beauty falls like silk rain on your up-turned face. We all know it. When what's gone slams and slices back to you in a dream, it makes a paper-doll, a parody, of any waking prayer.

Five cuts on the back of my ;*lkj* hand. Each cut stops my crying
when I'm at home. Each cut gives me something to look at. To see
& feel. A fine stream from beyond the boundary, 12 of your tears
along the *f* & *j* bones on the back of my hands. The solfa sight of
blood and the pinching sensation of the pain fit. Nothing else fits.
The pain of these little cuts is laughable. Local trivia. The salient
pain has no location on my body. I swim in it & I know most of
it belongs to people I don't know. Political. But at this moment
I can't touch that. It's existential, it touches you back. And it's
also racial. The world's a pitiful fucking liar. It moves like a long
wave I've ducked at the beach. Beyond the barriers beyond the
boundaries. The surface of my skin curves and tints brown like
a piece of paper before it bursts into flame. Sweet as ash in my
mouth. My breath smells like crushed stone, a first whiff of white
smoke from chalk burnt black.

These cuts are a perfectly rational behavior. Like good prose.
& perfectly meaningless. No object. Other cuts have healed
from previous bouts with breath stripped down to the color of
noonday sun on brushed steel. Together they've formed a glassy,
pale streak down the bones of my otherwise beige and olive-
toned hands.

I Google these cuts on my hands & find that we're called "cutters"
and most of us are adolescent girls. I smile. We really are what
we're not. One study has concluded that ritualized cutting "isn't
ever accompanied with suicidal ideation." Even better. More
proof that we think what we don't while we are what we aren't.

Last year, in May, I went to visit my sister in Colorado for the last time. I showed up with cuts lined up on both hands and spoke with authority about how and when she should die. She did. With my hand on her forehead. I felt the first wisp of cold come up from inside her face and instinctively and stupidly pulled up the covers under her chin.

The last time we spoke on the phone. You'd been involved with Michael who, when I was thirty-five, told me: "I've loved your sister for twenty-five years." He said, "Do you want to go fishing or have you ever fired an AK-47?" He looked at me and said, "I'm talking about love. Love means another's needs are more important than your own." I said, I think love means you can't tell one from the other. He smiled and said, "Come on, you'll love this. An AK is not actually a gun at all. It's the most viscous liquid ever created and a revolutionary tool the world over."

The last time we spoke on the phone you told me you'd broken up with Michael. He didn't like the comings and goings-on in your apartment. Your foot had swelled enough to break its bones. Your roommate had stolen your money and your food and your jeep. She brought back the jeep with the keys lost and the ignition toast. You've moved in above Chris B's studio. Now his son wants you out so he can have the loft for his new wife's yoga center. You say, Michael doesn't come around. You say: "I've got this fat little Navajo boy bringing me root beer whenever I want it." You say: "He's on his way up right now."

Of evicting you ten days before you died, Chris B's son tells me he's going to open a yoga school in your apartment. He tells me: "I want to prevent more people from becoming like your sister." My mouth moves without moving. I say, that shouldn't be too difficult.

On the phone, the last thing you ever said to me: "Look, I don't know what's wrong with Michael. He came in here, now he won't come back. I don't know what he thinks he saw, but that guy was *not* putting on his pants. Hey, got to go deary, my a-root beer-y is a-here-y. . .".

Salida, CO. Michael tells me he won a full scholarship to the
Art Institute of Chicago & so he joined the Navy and went to
Vietnam. By the time we talked he'd long been a successful
jeweler and maker of hot-air balloon ornaments out of recycled,
burnt-out light bulbs. He called that business "Balloonatics."
A few years later, he'd be swept up in a child sexual abuse
scandal and legal case that seemed patently false—economically
motivated, ridiculous—to me and everyone who knew him. In
the end it destroyed him, took everything but his talent & his
strange and quirky dignity. About the case Michael told me,
"look, I'm weird. But I'm not *that* weird." By 2020, Michael's been
dead for a number of years. On his grave and on my soul, I'd have
left my little children with him any day. And he loved my sister in
a real and truly imperfect way, unlike anyone else.

Soon after my sister's death. I asked Michael about you, Kate.

He said: "Your sister could be like a ray of sun come through the
clouds. The light alive in a July blizzard blown up off the Sangre
de Christo." He says, "when I got back from Vietnam, I lived in
a houseboat in Sausalito. It could be bright and sunny and, in
minutes, without warning, a fog could roll in that'd make you
wonder if you were standing and trying to lie down, or lying and
trying to stand up. You'd blink and all of a sudden, you don't
know if it's day or night? Summer or winter? Your sister could be
like *that*. Above all, we were all awed by her truly strange talent
and her perfect little body." That's what he said.

And he said: "I'd worked all day every day at my bench through most of three marriages. I'd be on my bench in the store and Kate'd pass by the open door. She'd always flash me something or other and I'd say to myself: 'Shit, Michael, no matter what you tell yourself, this does beat floating face down in the Mekong Delta.'"

I-80 E. I packed what I found of your work, eight canvasses, into your jeep and drove it across the country to NY. I love to drive for the simple illusion of motion. I found half the canvass roof and one back window. At night, Iowa swelled & rolled beneath me like a calm sea & smelled like deep green smoke. I see my hand on the wheel, the last wave of cuts almost healed.

Ca. 1975. When you were fourteen I was eight. Somehow Mom and Dad learned where you were living. I remember hearing it: "Steamboat Springs, Colorado?! Get a map." They called the police. They wanted you home. The police pin-pointed you. They picked you up and put you in jail. Dad came from a job somewhere, and you cursed him thru clenched teeth on the flight home. I remember, terrified of you, hiding upstairs while you hissed at our house as if it were prison. "You called the fucking cops on me?"

Rain in reverse. I remember one sentence from your return to us. Did I say I was stuck-to-the-wall terrified of you? You whispered low thru a smile like a straight razor on a strop, over and over at dinner: "You can't keep me here if I want to leave." I remember feeling like you'd etched the sentence in the air with fingernails full of flesh carved out of your arms. You were right. You were gone in a week. A month? All I remember is that one sentence of your hissing & evil teenage flesh hanging there before my eyes, the only living thing in the terrified room. The sound of flesh that's declared itself uncaged. I can taste that sentence whenever I want. It's under my tongue. It tastes like sweat off clean brass. Like adrenaline.

Down the street from Denver Medical Center, Mom, Mary, and I eat lunch. Two blocks up on the fourth floor, a machine jerks your chest open. I realize she's talking about your return from Steamboat when she asks if we remember going to a family counselor at the mental health hospital where you were an inpatient for a month. Mary nods. A dim bulb lights up a room in my head. Mom tells us that, after the meeting, the doctor asked dad, "Well, your daughter's clearly not 'ill.' What do *you* think we should do?" To which, dad: "Hell, you're the goddamned experts, how the hell do I know what to do?" Mom smiles over her burrito, says it's one of his favorite stories.

I look at Mary, "have you ever heard *that* one?" She shakes her head. I look back at Mom.

[   ]

On November 29, 1928, Hart Crane wrote to Yvor Winters and told him to stop pushing him to write back. Crane wrote: "I've been encircled too much by the whirlwind hysterics of– well, Fate. (If one may allude to one's family in that way) to answer your last. And it isn't possible now, either."

The first line in Crane's first book is:

> As silent as a mirror is believed
> Realities plunge in silence by. . .

Denver I.C.U. I mean this to say exactly what it says. I mean nothing by way of inference. Thick folio stock. Let's pretend there's nothing behind this page but the shadow of the fingers that hold it.

It's not a lie to say that Mary repeatedly talked about having to see the finals of American Idol on the day of your death. Mary and I spent one day together at opposite sides of your bed. If there are opposites, which I doubt, here we are. The pain killers gradually dissipated and you became agitated, still not conscious. We stood there holding your arms and legs back from entanglement in the metal lifts on the hospital bed. It's true that my mind tells my body it can still feel my hand on your leg. Your hand, rough, *your* hand, Kate, Jesus, nails black from the inside-out with blood, warm in mine. My sister's warmth. My sister's living body. The warmth that covered me like a thin nude sheet. What they dragged back to burn down the house in my terrified eight-year-old head.

I hear your voices behind my ear.

Salida, CO. Your diary. On the cover you'd written *Deeds and Appointments*. One of two entries in words among the images: "May, 2004 ---- 5:45 am. I'm just getting to bed... Reason-
----things (my things) are slipping out of alignment. Bit of background-----for the last few years. I've aloud my heart to govern my conscience and side step reason in the name of love. (needless to say) My life, health, finances, and finally basic order including [illegible] have suffered to near death for Kate.

"Since I'm still breathing, I thought it might be time to straighten things up a bit. My health has taken over my government. If I stray for a day, my feet blow up, eyes turn to gold-----If I keep stepping in the wrong direction, it seems as if even the air is as a brick wall, etc----- Not a question of good or bad, just gotta stay on Kate's tiny narrow path, personally destined for me, to have abundant life with the glow from my love's smile radiating causing my countenance to beam with the wonderful Bright life and love of God. Thank you Lord for directing my path. I will wake when you awe me with your praise, flowing from my soul as a perfectly directed symphony!

"Lord please surround me and mine with endless grace. Be with me in my dreams as the Love of my life—touch me close from flesh all the way to my spirit and soul I give you power over my body while I rest. Yes Lord, touch me. [Sketches] Good night (6:15)"

Denver I.C.U. Your skin's patina mummifies you. I touch you
with breath as if with an archaeologist's brush. You seem ancient,
utterly beyond. I touch you again. Love scraped clean from the
bone. I touch you the way I touch my baby girl at bedtime. Forever.
Alchemy. Fingertips burned somehow clean of the in-born disgust
for ourselves, the basic fear of pain already alive within us, pain
that holds us back from touching each other.

I think to myself, Pavese had it wrong. Sure, the thing most feared in secret always happens. But, that's because by the time you fear it, it's actually *already* happened. If not, fear would be a more useful emotion. I hear a padded scuffle and a crash of metal pans down the hall. I look up and the intern's picking himself up off the floor again.

It's not a lie to say that the feel of your skin burned Mary's hands. Her touch is forced and made mostly of recoil. It's not a lie to say that she needs to evade the reality on its back between us. You. Within us you're different people. She can show the scars on her forearms from your teenage nails. The wars I watched having no idea what they were about. But I know they don't still feel like scars to her now. Worse than pain. They tingle & bristle with numb heat. She'd rather not feel the tingles of her flesh and blood on its back in this bed. You, Kate. I feel them too. A force of life. For her chaos and pain and panic. The easy and endless evidence points in both directions at once.

If there's blame in this account, it's the reader's blame. Not mine. The contempt for our failure to be more of ourselves than the barriers and boundaries of so-called experience allow? That's mine. The despair over this avoidance of contradiction, our devotion to the idea that one basic element can elide another? That's mine. If there's love for the countless drapes, like lace onto its shadow, of translucent gauze in the human psyche? You can call that mine, Kate, but I got the first hint of it from you.

My hands drink your skin. You never hurt *my* body. My body's tattooed with brush tones of pleasure and mystery. You invaded my brain like a viral kind of love. You taught me terror at first-hand, fingertip by fingertip. Meter. Syllable by syllable, you held the ends of your hair and painted the great rivers of the world, Nile, Ganges, Tigris, Yangtze, down the backs of my bare, hairless legs. You opened me. You'd say your nipples were softer than a darkness held by a blind man in the palm of his hand. You'd pin me to my bed with stories and songs and drawings of that dead-stick thin white girl with hair between her teeth. You said, in her house she had a chopping block the shape of a human being. I must have been very little, I didn't know that word. I remember wondering, human bean? Your friend with the ankle stuck in the river mud like a white stake in Dracula's black heart. You sing me her song, "I'm going to eat you for sup-per..." Your eyes blaze.

You'd torn the windows out of our house. I'd grown up in the
shattered remains of an attempt at something. An empty yard.
Today I'd call it American whiteness. You destroyed it before
my eyes before it had a chance to exist—at least for me, in
me—at all. By the time they were re-building it, if that's what
happened, I was gone. Of course, it's always being re-built
everywhere. But that'd never be home to me.

Your absence and the flesh chandelier of your voice, left the
myth of parental knowing and control, hanging dead from
a noose in the wide-open front door. You blew off the door,
Kate, everyone followed. Mom went to work, then to school,
then more school, then more work. Mary left to college & on
to life. Dad was always gone. *Chicago, the city that works.* I
can't remember when he left for real for the first time. I wasn't
born. *A man's got to work.* I can't remember a day when I
didn't feel torn open and lost in those houses of theirs. But
she stayed.

The little cannibal in my brain with my name in her mouth
sits with me, even today, in any and every empty room I'm in.
Empty, meaning I'm alone as well, as empty meaning all the
empty rooms full of white people that'd never be home to me.
Your rhythms surround me like a bell ringing underwater.
Invisible music. Like living tendrils of terror like the hair-thin
white roots we found under all the flagstones we'd upturn in

81

the alley. ~~Something of you transmits in every sense I have.~~
My touch—as much yours as mine—a kind of contempt for
boundaries, for borders.

As I got older I found it's not like that for everyone. For some
people, I'd learn, touch is the prayer of division, and protection.

[   ]

From the first, I'd been uneasy with how Mary couldn't come within an emotional mile of your hospital bed. True. I needed a chair in the first moments after we arrived. I was dizzy. In a minute, the invisible tendrils found each other in the air, my dizziness left. You weren't alone in that room anymore. You were not alone with me in that room and you knew it. Or felt it. I'm not alone right now, late night in this abandoned house, in this abandoned upstate town, eye to eye with my impossible reflection in the flat clear pane of wind coming thru this wide-open window.

One day, months before you ended up in Denver I.C.U., things were really bad. Bones in your feet broken from swelling—Mary actually said you could come stay with her. It was a lot for her to tell you that. And you said: "Ok, but only if I'm absolutely positive I'm going to die."

And dad stayed in Croatia. I know he told you things from there. I don't know what he said. I know he planted a white rose bush the day you died. Mom told me, of course.

Whereabouts unknown. I can see dad replaying those nights alone on the road in the 70s. Winters meant migration, meant curry-scented motels in the South. Pacing back and forth in his head. Dying to get back to the job for the simple excuse to get on his knees. He worked almost nose to the floor. I'd see that later. He dying to get back to where he could blame the ache in his hands on the brick. This was his gift to us; it transmits too, and differently in all three of us. Three of us: what a thought.

Denver I.C.U. It's decided that you'll die tomorrow. I call dad. I use the pay phone down in the hospital lobby. He answers. 3:30 am his time on Krk. "You sleep?": "No": "What are you doing?": "Sitting here, lying here, I don't know. What's the prognosis?": "There isn't one, Dad": "Well, Hell." Silence. "I want to thank you for being there, Ed": "Of course": "So long, Ed." So long, Dad.

Whipped by the huge surf of the unsaid & me thinking it's only unsaid in *my* head. Outside my flesh, the unsaid doesn't exist at all. Me thinking: no transcendence. Me thinking: throw a brick at a window and watch it vanish as it hits the pane. Me thinking: that's the sound of the unsaid. This deep lace of timpani; the slide of cymbal lip across my eyes.

Me thinking family: what an ocean, what an intricate room.

He told mom to buy you a box of chocolate cherries. She got one in the Zagreb airport. He meant that, Kate. He really meant it. Of course you couldn't eat them and so I kept them. Each cherry sits in a plastic pod, wrapped in aluminum skin. I looked them up. One of these words on the box, I forget which, is the Croatian word for "delicious."

I think the following in lucid prose. A clear, stainless pool without any blame or malice. It's intensity without an object that carries the question through my lips: "What kind of monsters are we?" Your little girl's dying, your sister's dying. We can disappear from the world without a word made flesh even from our own families? Mom tried. But her training is really in the obliteration of unhappy things. Oblivion is beyond her. Give her that. Mom tried.

I mean only this. I mean nothing by way of inference. That cannibal little girl you made up raised me. It's she who introduces me to every living person I meet. I know it now; from *my* version of the story: she leaves the living to me; she only eats the walking dead.

My mother read this book. I sent it to Croatia in a moment of delusion. She called me and a white blade came from her mouth. I love her. She said, "I'll see to it that your father never reads this." I love her. We lived alone for half my life in their world (white). She told me this, as my mother, with the will (white) and tone (white) of obliteration in her voice. I think oblivion is an inalienable right of the human interior, a fundamental otherness we house that answers to no one including ourselves. In Visconti's *The Leopard*, someone says that peasants know this about oblivion and that they crave it. My mother's will (white) to obliteration (white) is the denial of this sacred oblivion. As I often do, I hear Baldwin's voice talking about "a level of experience that Americans deny." I think, this is one small twig (white) of a branch reaching from a limb (white) ultimately rooted in this denial (white). The denial (white) of oblivion. I love her and she loved me. Before I was 18, we lived alone together for years. She never left. She could only be there as far as she could, but she never left. I think my mother meant this obliteration to protect herself, and us, and me. And, maybe it did, up to a point. But beyond that (what?), protection isn't protection; we find others who go with us.

I-80. Kate, let's you and I call it traded fours, two days around Salida in search of the roof of your jeep. The more I looked the less I found. Two unopened syringes under the driver's seat. Under the passenger's floor mat, the license plate: FDL 465. Colorado.

Thunderheads explode a few hundred miles to my right. Let's call it sixteen hours under a blue sky in May & let's allow that it's all downhill into Omaha. & this late-night set's the first jazz I've heard in days. From my side of this sixteen-hour slope, it sounds like four bars of vanity & din. Maybe eight bars. I know better. I've ridden downhill before. I know lots of stuff. It took Billie Holiday forty-four years and several months to live her way thru *her* liver's final flutter and half-tones.

Driving tonight I think: Well, you beat her, Kate. Beat her by at
least a month. Fair and square but let's call it a tie. Like the roof
and the license, like fencing Mom with disappearing syringes, let's
call it dead even. Even you said it, Kate, last year when I asked you
about it, "You just don't move to the top of a continent this size to
keep some damned roof on your car." The heat blasting past us &
out the roofless jeep. This jeep. Smoke from your squinted mouth
a basket of snakes into the Milky Way just above Leadville. Here
I am cloned to I-80 East, lightning off into the purple to the south
at my right. I hit search on the radio & the red numbers blur. I
look back to the right into a black blast of Blakey & I don't know
the year, the tune, or the horn player though it's probably Morgan.
I know you know as much about something like this as you'd ever
find out right away.

I know it's black, blasted, & Blakey and I know no one knows which is which? It's not a thought or a voice that hits me out the dark sky over what'll all too soon be Iowa as Colorado (without you in it?) slips farther and farther uphill behind me. I wonder how fast I'd have to go until the wind would suck me from the seat & I'd let go of the wheel & spend a few seconds with Blakey & never get home & never kiss my daughter with Colorado on the rear plate in the front seat & you dead & that whole high state empty of me meaning empty of you. That state with no *me* in it? I don't know nothing about that. Then it hits me & I hear Billie Holiday say "go ahead, Art, Work!" & I know it's not Billie Holiday who said that but Mingus on Debut.

It's not this record & it wasn't a voice and I know it doesn't matter, either. I wonder why, mouth wide open & full of smoke from bonfires on what seems like all the farms in the uphill county coming up off the Missouri River. Why? Why change Mingus to Holiday and back? I ask this out loud when my eyes fall on the speed dials. The cell phone tells me I've missed another call & I see this jeep's been driven exactly 53035 miles & I see that someone at some point punched the trip-lever-thing under the odometer. Whoever that was, Kate, & wherever they were, I see it was exactly eight-hundred eighty-eight miles from here. If it was you, I know you were exactly that far from here. If it wasn't you who did it, I know you were somewhere else. 53053 on the dial. Billie and you dead at 44 and some change. Eight-hundred eighty-eight miles on the trip-dial ... Point what? I wait for one more eight. The horn trades a four with the drums & my eyes trade it back to the road.

For most of my life, Kate, each time we've met alone, you tell me that dad cried on the plane ride from Steamboat when they found you and he dragged you home. You say, "have you ever seen dad cry?" I say no. You say, "*I* have." There's something of a boast in it. There's nothing left of your terrible teenage maliciousness in it—or, from what I can see, in you. But every time you tell me this, I strangely resent you. I can feel a thought murmur, somehow bitterly, but the translation's false: "a 40-whatever-year-old woman, she can paint a face out of thin air, in sugar spilled on a mahogany bar and *this* is her achievement." Maybe that's the thought, but if I'm honest, it's likely closer to: "my kids will never ask each other *that*—"

You say dad never wanted to work. You say that's why all he ever talked about is work. You say people hold U-turns inside themselves. I think, "U-turns in cul-de-sacs, Kate." But, I say nothing. You say "dad wanted to do what *I* did: walk out to the highway with an easel on his back and hitch a ride."

With that in mind, a few things come into focus. You two face to face, the pure pitch and white light of extremity eyes itself in the mirror. It falls away, ever-deeper into itself. "I think I'll eat one of those chocolate covered cherries."

The Angel of Mt. Shavano is a glacier. The winter snows melt
away each year and reveal her. It's supposed to be an "Indian
Legend" that, born of her sorrow, her tears come down the
mountain each year to swell the rivers and irrigate the valley.
I don't know the exact origin of the legend. But it scans a few
degrees too Catholic for the figure visible from Salida in May.
Her arms flung out, head pitched to the side, hips bumping
a-kilter, I think: tears? Prove it.

The Angel of Mt. Shavano,
in May, Chaffee County, Colorado

Last time I saw you on your feet, we climbed Mt. Shavano to have lunch on the angel's hip. Year by year step by step you led me up past the line where trees grow past the line where shrubs cling to rocks & you tell south by the lichen. I hesitate when my lungs begin to ache, lose a full step for your every two. We pass the line where grizzlies plunder pinecone stores of black cat-eared alpine squirrels. Empty craters that smell of thin green air. We're into the zone of the all too recently disturbed stones where grizzlies find moths that blow in off the plains of Kansas and Nebraska to mate in the rubble beyond the tree-line. I don't want to know any of this, but I do. You do too but could give a damn. I'm scared & can't breathe. I join the invisible crowd & turn back and let you go & you're bears be damned on all fours now. I sit on a boulder & gasp for air & I see you get smaller & smaller & with each blink I can see it clearly. You could care less about the glacier angel up the slope. You used to tell me I made you safe because when kidnappers came they'd take the youngest. The boy. Now I'm bigger than you are, so, here I am. & there you are, your liver floating in the numbbright, curled up like a peach pit on a hissing radiator, eyes alight with the flamedark torch in each pulse. & there you go, a slow drip of Patrón & a quick whiff of nicotine for lunch as you search for the line up beyond which elevation the lungs change to birds & you can go on living without having to have a body at all

Denver I.C.U. Here's my hand holding onto yours. Here's
the tattooed wedding ring you got at Sturgis. Third husband,
forth marriage. Here's the voice of the best man from your first
wedding in Vegas. He stands at the table in The Landmark.
1975. There you are, just turned 15, Mrs. Tony Latore. Me, mom,
you, and ten real live high rollers at the dinner. Mom paid. And
the best man, a pit boss in whatever casino, raises his Scotch that
mom bought: "here's to Kate and Tony, and to Mrs. Pavlick, you
haven't gotten rid of a problem, ma'am, you've gained one."

Here's an orderly come to plunge the blood and yellow fluid
draining from your lungs. Here's my hand, full of scars. I'm fresh
here from the college that's killing me if that's what it is and it
isn't. A single line of cuts along the bone to the knuckle of my left
index finger. Cuts I put there nightly to remind myself I'm alive in
a world that convinced itself to die, stenciled a smile on its skull,
and kept walking around like nothing happened.

Of what I wrote about you, Kate, a living person (now dead too), a friend I trust wrote me the following. "Let it go where it goes. . . But I'm not talking about therapy, friend." In a poem called "The Blood Is Justified," Muriel Rukeyser urges the reader to "treat the wound with laceration." In another, more public piece, my friend writes that "women have often felt insane when cleaving to the truth of our experience." You read none of this. You knew all these things. You knew them in ways at once beyond & within knowing, in ways elemental and indistinguishable from your daily life. In other words, you *knew* none of this. You had it in a heavy way, in the reckless core of each cell in your body.

Like a swipe of soft lead, an unknown veers into being.

These are reader's notes, then. Mine. I'll burn them and stir the ash in with your own before I stir part of you into the headwaters of the Arkansas River. The rest goes with Chris B on his bike; in an unfinished nook of Bishop's Castle; and some, one day, to the frozen hip of the Angel.

Chris B's likely too decent to tell me this, but I know he's a
relatively hairy man. And I don't know who suggested it. Whose
fetish? I know, one night, under candles, you lay him down and
shaved every hair from his body. From his toes up his legs to his
balding gray head. Your hands smoothed the lather and the razor
traced every hairy nook he had.

He's too decent to say this. He's in love with life. I've seen him
dance his way to a distilled happiness that could float a lead pipe
in thin mountain air. Over salt rimmed eyes, when you died, he
told me that he knows a parent's grief for a dead child.

He won't say he tingled & quivered beneath your blade. But,
he did. On that bed in his cabin under that light, he felt like a
woman had shaved the inside of his skin clean. He lay there in
the dark, smoke tailing off the wicks around his bed, perfectly
nude, hairless, as if newborn, for the first and probably the last
time in his life. Chris B knows what I know. If you touched
someone, Kate, they stayed touched.

Bubbles of oblivion. A year and one month after your death we all sat in the Riverside Park along the Arkansas in Salida. A few people were there. The wind came up that afternoon and blew clouds of dust north along Route 50 down from Monarch Pass. We blew thousands of bubbles through the air. I watched the soap-seals find their spheres in the sunlight and blink back into nothing. The huge ones left an instant's rainbow.

My Dad, our Dad, blowing bubbles.

I brought your ashes to the riverbank and poured the cloud of you into the clear, cold speed of the river. I looked to my left & thought about the spot where Chris B.'s son drowned. A game his brother invented where you tie a rope to the bridge and hold onto it while you surf the rapids. It's the inventor— the brother who lived—who evicted you for his yoga school. I scooped out a Ziploc's worth of you to give to Chris B and told him to let you fly on his cycle at 90 mph. He says, at times on his bike on an unknown road, he has to scream out of pure elation while he rides. He'll do it.

Mary with bubbles and Milan and Suci and Stacey with bubbles.

With my right arm, I reach into the river to wipe the heavy, white shards of bone off the stones and you go and the water washes you from my fingers. The knuckles on my left hand are still dry and covered with grayish-blue powder. At one point, bringing my hand to my face, I realize that you smell like you again. I realize that human ash smells sweet, a thickened-smooth lavender. Ash gone to cream in my nose. My sister. And grief. And, bubbles.

I walk the park thru shadows winded wild and monotone stabs of light

I turned around at the end of the park. I kept walking. Back at the riverbank, Sunčana, age five, kisses my cheek and puts her hands on my hot shoulders. She turns my face toward her. She says, "Daddy, why'd you come back?" I say, "that's the thing, Suci, no one ever gets to know that."

The orderly silently says, "sorry," and plunges out more fluid. It's not his fault. Your hand is warm and sweats in my palm like a tiny glove. Warm. Your touch is still alive in my hand. It doesn't smell like yours anymore. He leaves. Your skin smells like chemicals. You lie on your back and a tear-drop of blood seeps from under your eyelid. It sits on your cheek like a red deer over a high fence. I lean down & blow on it gently until I think I can see it take a breath on its own.

Here's my *asdf* hand holding onto your leathery skin, paint still under your nails. My other arm under the sheet holds you behind your knee, the length of my forearm the inverse slope of your calf. Spoons stored in the drawer.

The newest cuts on my hands are a few days old for the first time in weeks. Which means you haven't been alone in days. Me either. Somewhere, someone you created is watching this. One of us is healing, Kate, and one's dying. If I had a third hand I'd take a penny from your purse. I'd watch your eye opalesce it as it flipped. I'd close my eyes and let you call it in the air.

"Untitled," Kate Pavlich, Undated

Sunčana Pavlić

ED PAVLIĆ's twelfth and most recent book is *Outward: Adrienne Rich's Expanding Solitudes* (University of Minnesota Press, 2021). *Another Kind of Madness: A Novel* (Milkweed Editions) appeared in paperback in April 2020. He is Distinguished Research Professor of English and African American Studies at the University of Georgia.

milkweed
editions

Founded as a nonprofit organization in 1980, Milkweed Editions
is an independent publisher. Our mission is to identify, nurture
and publish transformative literature, and build an engaged
community around it.

Milkweed Editions is based in Bdé Óta Othúŋwe (Minneapolis)
within Mní Sota Makhóčhe, the traditional homeland of
the Dakhóta people. Residing here since time immemorial,
Dakhóta people still call Mní Sota Makhóčhe home, with four
federally recognized Dakhóta nations and many more Dakhóta
people residing in what is now the state of Minnesota. Due to
continued legacies of colonization, genocide, and forced removal,
generations of Dakhóta people remain disenfranchised from
their traditional homeland. Presently, Mní Sota Makhóčhe has
become a refuge and home for many Indigenous nations and
peoples, including seven federally recognized Ojibwe nations.
We humbly encourage our readers to reflect upon the historical
legacies held in the lands they occupy.

milkweed.org

Milkweed Editions also gratefully acknowledges sustaining support from our Board of Directors; the Alan B. Slifka Foundation and its president, Riva Ariella Ritvo-Slifka; the Amazon Literary Partnership; the Ballard Spahr Foundation; *Copper Nickel*; the McKnight Foundation; the National Endowment for the Arts; the National Poetry Series; the Target Foundation; and other generous contributions from foundations, corporations, and individuals. Also, this activity is made possible by the voters of Minnesota through a Minnesota State Arts Board Operating Support grant, thanks to a legislative appropriation from the arts and cultural heritage fund. For a full listing of Milkweed Editions supporters, please visit milkweed.org.

Interior design by Tijqua Daiker and Mary Austin Speaker
Typeset in Adobe Jenson

Adobe Jenson was designed by Robert Slimbach for Adobe
and released in 1996. Slimbach based Jenson's roman styles on a
text face cut by fifteenth-century type designer Nicolas Jenson,
and its italics are based on type created by Ludovico Vicentino
degli Arrighi, a late fifteenth-century papal
scribe and type designer.